ON DREAMS

BY

SAINT SYNESIOS

Translated, With Notes,

BY

ISAAC MYER.

ONE HUNDRED COPIES PUBLISHED BY THE TRANSLATOR.

PHILADELPHIA.
1888.

The following translation of the Treatise, On Dreams, by Saint Synesios, with brief notes; was published by me in, The Platonist, Vol. IV., Nos., 4, 5 and 6: and one hundred copies struck off for my use. The printing office of that Periodical is at Osceola, St. Clair County, Missouri, and owing to the disadvantage of distance I did not have an opportunity to correct the proofs, I have therefore annexed the following errata.

P. 1, for "MEYÈR" r., MYER.
" 3, l., 26, r., flight.
" 5, l., 17, r., for "a," an; l., 18, r., because; l., 32, beg., r., they.
" 7, l., 26, r., and arouses it to pass
" 8, l., 29, for "of" r., to
" 12, l., 1 for "lakes" r., takes; note, l., 8, r., probably.
" 14, last two lines, r., who born free, inflamed by the beauty of a slave, sell themselves for a time, and in order to remain near the one, etc.
" 16, note, last line, r., *Nephesh*.
" 17, l., 16 and 17, r., celestial.
" 19 l., 4 fr. bottom r., nocturnal.
" 20, l., 20, r., acquire; l., 29 r., we should do
" 21, l., 3, for "Some" r., The; l., 4, r., triarchs; l., 18 and 19, r., between; l., 24 instead of "it thus" r., thus it; l., 27 for "the" r., an.
" 22, l., 18, strike out "the."
" 23, l., 4, r., tyrant.
" 24, l, 26, r., speaking.
" 25, l., 10, strike out "is."
" 26, l, 26, beg., r., then.
" 27, l., 26, for "conjectures" r., conjunctures.
" 28, note, r., *Me-qor 'Hai-yeem*.
" 32, l., 10, r., entirely; l., 28, r., careful.
" 34, l., 19, r., spheres.

PHILADELPHIA:
No. 929 CLINTON STREET.

ON DREAMS

BY

SYNESIOS.*

Translated with Notes,

BY

ISAAC MEYER.

PREFACE.

A very ancient custom, and one which Plato especially uses, is to conceal under the form of a familiar subject the most serious teachings of philosophy; so that the truths the discovery of which has been most difficult will not again escape from the memory of men nor, being disseminated, receive the contaminations of the profane vulgar. Such is the design that I propose in this book. Whether my work conforms in all its parts to the antique mode of writing I leave to the judgment of industrious and enlightened readers.

alleg-

I.

THE PROPHETIC FACULTY IS THE NOBLEST SUBJECT OF STUDY FOR MAN.

If dreams prophesy the future, if visions which present themselves to the mind during sleep afford some *indicia* whereby to divine future things, dreams will be at the same time true and obscure, and even in their

*Synesios of Cyrene was born of a noble family *circa* A. D. 370, in Cyrene, a city of the Libyan Pentapolis, Egypt. At first a heathen he subsequently became a Christian. About 398 he became a pupil at Alexandria of the celebrated Hypatia. In 409 was made Bishop of Ptolemais which he did not accept till 410. He died *circa* 413 A. D. He is best known through his Hymns.

The Roman Catholic Church canonized him as St. Synesios.

obscurity the truth will reside. "The Gods with a thick veil have covered human life."*

To obtain things of the greatest value without labor is a happiness which appertains only to the gods; but by men not only virtue but all blessings "can alone be achieved by sweat (labor)."† Now the prophetic power is the greatest of goods: it is through knowledge and the gnostic faculty that God differs from man, and man from the brute. God knows all by virtue of His own nature, but man by the aid of the prophetic power may add much to his natural knowledge. The vulgar man knows only the present; that which is future he can only conjecture. Kalkhas alone in the assembly of all the Greeks apprehended "the present, the future and the past."‡ In Homer, Zeus regulates the affairs of the gods, because he was "born first, and therefore knows more;"§ because knowledge is the privilege of the aged. If the poet thus recalls Zeus' age, it is because the years bring with them that wisdom to which nothing else can be compared. If we think, from other passages, that the supremacy of Zeus was the result of the vigor of his arms, because Homer said, "He carried it by force," ‖—we do not understand poetry, and cannot grasp the philosophy which it encloses, viz., that the gods are no other than pure Intelligences. After saying that Zeus is very strong, the poet immediately adds that he is the oldest, which signifies that Zeus is the oldest Intelligence. But the vigor of intelligence, is this any other thing than wisdom? Whoever may be the god who rules the other gods, it is because he is wise that he reigns. Because he is superior in wisdom, "he carries it by force," signifies that he knows

*Hesiod. The Works and Days, 42.

†*Ibid.* 287.

‡Iliad, i, 70.

§Ibid. xiii, 355.

‖*Ibid*, xv, 165

more than the others. The sage has then a species of affiinity with God, because he endeavors to approach Him by the faculty of knowledge, and exerts himself about intuitive thought which is the essence of God. These facts show plainly that one of the most noble subjects of research for man is the prophetic faculty.

II.

THE UNIVERSE IS AN ANIMATED EXISTENCE WHICH IS CONNECTED TOGETHER IN ALL ITS PARTS. THE DIFFERENT KINDS OF PROPHESY.

All things, by their relation to each other, can give omens; because all together they are only different parts of one animal, the Universe.* The Universe may be compared to a book in which are inscribed letters of every description, such as Phœnician, Egyptian and Assyrian: the wise man deciphers these letters; and he is really wise who learns by and from nature, and another is wise in other things—this one more, and the other less. Thus for example one merely learns the syllables, another apprehends the general style, a third comprehends the whole discourse. Wise men see beforehand that which may happen; some by regarding the planets, others the fixed stars, others the comets and fires which traverse space. Some also prophesy by inspecting the entrails of victims or by listening to the songs of birds, or through watching their flight and their haunts. There are other omens by the aid of which they can predict the future, as words, or fortunate meetings; all are able to draw prognostications from everything. If a bird had our intelligence, man would serve it, as the bird serves man, for knowledge and divination: because we are as to them that which they are as to us, a race which, always renewing itself and as old as the world, is entirely qualified to give signs.

*This is the doctrine of the Makrokosm and Mikrokosm.

Ne.

Artem.

III.

ALL THINGS HAVE A MUTUAL AFFINITY AND ACT UPON EACH OTHER.

It was necessary that all the parts of this grand whole, animated with a common life, should be united by an intimate relation, as members of the same body.

It is thus perhaps that we may be able to explain the enchantments by magicians: because as there are omens in nature, attractions also exist. The wise man is he who knows how all things are bound together in this world; he makes one thing come to him through the intermediary of another thing; with the assistance of the present objects he extends his power over the most distant objects; he works by means of words, figures, and material substances.

In ourselves the suffering of one organ communicates itself to other organs; a pain in the finger or the foot sometimes brings a tumor in the groin, while all the intermediary organs do not suffer anything: it is because the groin and the foot both belong to the same body and have their especial relations. Among the gods who are in this world, there are some who have affinities and sympathies with certain stones and certain plants, and these affinities are such that by and through these stones or plants they may be attracted. In the same way the musician who produces the "*hypate*" adds to that note not the nearest note to it, but the "*epitrite*" and the "*nete*."*

And this arises from the ancient homogeneity (harmony) of things. At present there is between the different parts, as in a family, dissimilarity; because the

*Τὴν ὑπάτην, the *hypate*, the gravest note. Τὴν ἐπόγδοον, the next note, which is an octave higher, and which gives with the *hypate* a discord corresponding to the affinity of 8 to 9. Τὴν ἐπιτρίτην, the *epitrite*, a note which will give with the hypate a chord analogous to the affinity of 4 to 8, the consonance to the fifth. Τὴν νήτην, *nete*, which is the most elevated note, gives with the *hypate* a consonance with the octave analogous to the affinity of 2 to 1.

world is not a simple unity, but a composite unity. The elements therefore sometimes are in accord, at other times are in conflict; but their strife always results in the harmony of the whole. So the sounds which the lyre gives are an assemblage of dissonances and consonances: it is from contraries that the unity is born, which makes of the lyre, as of the universe, a well ordered whole.

IV.

THIS RECIPROCAL ACTION OF THINGS CAN ONLY BE EXERCISED IN THE WORLD. OBSCURITY IS ESSENTIAL TO DIVINATION.

Archimedes, the Sicilian, asked for a fulcrum situated outside of the earth to move the earth, saying: "Whilst I inhabit it I cannot act upon it." But it is entirely different with those who penetrate the mysteries of the world, and thus acquire a portion of the divinatory or prophetic science: if such a one was placed outside of the world, he could not any longer use his knowledge; becouse he exercises it upon the world, and by means of the world. Going out of our universe, you will look in vain: from the observation of the phenomena which are produced above the region in which the soul is diffused you will not apprehend anything. Over that which is divine, outside of the world, magic has no power. "He abides by himself, free of all care he is utterly regardless of it."*

Intuitive reason (*νους*) is essentially independent: it must become passive before it can be influenced by enchantments. The multiplicity of beings included in the world, and the affinities existing between them, give birth to all kinds of divination and mysteries; different because they are many, but by virtue of their affinities are really one great whole. It is not expedient to speak inconsiderately of the mysteries, by reason of our respect for the laws of the State; but it is permissible to

*Iliad. xv 106.

explain divination or the prophetic power. We have eulogized that art in general; we will now consider especially the most perfect of all divinations. They all present the common characteristic of obscurity; the attentive contemplation of the things of this world will not help in any way to dissipate this obscurity. Obscurity, as we shall see, is essential to divination, as mystery is to the sacred initiations. It is thus that the oracle of Delphi is not comprehended by all because it expresses itself in ambiguous terms; and when the gods pointed out to the Athenians how they would be able to save themselves, the assembled people could not have grasped the meaning of its words, if Themistokles had not been there to explain them. Thus we must not reject divination through dreams because, in common with all divination and the oracles, it has obscurity.

V.

OF INTELLECT, SOUL, REASON, AND IMAGINATION.

Of all disciplines we should specially study that which is of us, and within us, and the peculiar property of each soul. Intellect or Intuitive Reason (νους) contains in itself the images of the things which are real, as the ancient philosophy teaches; we may add that the soul contains images of things which are becoming (contingent). There is then, between intellect and the soul, the same affinity as between the absolute and contingent. We will invert the order of the terms. We will join the first to the third, the second to the fourth: the proportions will still remain true, as knowledge demonstrates to us. It will thus be established that the soul, as we have advanced, contains in itself the images of the things which become. It encloses them wholly, but it produces them outwardly only at a convenient time; imagination is similar to a mirror in which it reflects itself, so that the animal may perceive the images which have their seats in the soul. We are not conscious of these actions of the intellect, so long as the governing faculty does not reveal them to us, all that which it ignores escapes the knowledge of the animal; in the same manner we are not able to grasp any idea of the things which are in the first soul* so long as the imagination does not receive the images. This imaginative life is an inferior life, a particular condition of our nature. The senses are present to it: we see colors, we hear sounds, we touch and grasp objects, although our corporeal organs remain inactive; perhaps in this state our perceptions are more pure. It is thus that we often enter into conversation with the gods: they warn us, answer us, and give to us useful advice. So that I am not surprised that some have owed to a sleep the discovery of a treasure; and that one may have gone to sleep very ignorant, and after having had in a dream a conversation with the Muses, awakened an able poet, which has happened in my time to some, and in which there is nothing strange. I do not speak of those who have had, in their sleep, the revelation of a danger which threatened them, or the knowledge of a remedy that would cure them. But when sleep opens the way to the most perfect inspections of true things to the soul which previously had not desired these inspections, nor thought concerning the ascent to intellect —and arouses it to pass beyond nature and reunite itself to the intelligible sphere from which it has wandered so far that it does not now know even from whence it came,—*this*, I say, is most marvellous and obscure.

VI.

THE POWER OF IMAGINATION, WHICH IS PRE-EMINENTLY THE UNDERSTANDING.

If one thinks it extraordinary that the soul may thus

*Synesios holds to the idea of several divisions of the spiritual. By the "governing faculty" it is necessary to understand Reason or Wisdom. The first division is the Rational soul, in opposition to the soul evident to the Senses, the Vegetative Soul. The Qabbalists divided the spiritual into three main divisions, *Neshamah* higher soul, *Ruach* spirit, and *Nephesh* vital soul. The first, the highest, they divided into two others still more idealized.

ascend to the superior region, and does not believe that the way to this felicitous union lies through the imagination, let him hear the sacred oracles when they speak about the different roads which lead to the higher sphere. After enumerating the various *subsidia* which help the ascent of the soul by arousing and developing its powers, they say

> "By lessons some are enlightened,
> By sleep others are inspired."*

You see the distinction which the oracle establishes: upon the one side, inspiration; upon the other, study; the former it says is instruction whilst one is awake, the latter when asleep. Whilst awake, it is always a man who is the instructor; but when asleep, it is from God that the knowledge comes. They know from the first all that which is taught to them; because in giving knowledge thus God does not instruct in the usual manner. These facts are set forth to show the excellence of the imaginative life to those who do not esteem it. I am not astonished at their opinion: through their superabundant wisdom they are attached to practices condemned by the sacred oracles, for the oracles say:

> "Sacrifices and victims
> Are only vain amusements."†

The oracles advise us to renounce such things. But the men of whom I speak, being superior to the multitude in their own opinion, practice almost all kinds of divination. However they neglect divination by dreams, a method within the reach of all, alike of the ignorant and the wise. But why! Does not the wise man know better that which is common to all? Almost all good things, and especially the most precious, are the common property of humanity. In the universe nothing is more magnificent and divine than the sun, nor more

*Sibylline Oracles.
†Sibylline Oracles.

common. It is a great happiness to behold God; but to know God by means of the imagination is a higher intuition. Imagination is the sense of the senses, necessary to all others; it inheres at the same time in both the soul and the body.* It dwells within us: established in the head, as in a citadel which nature has built for us, and it governs the animal life. The hearing and the sight are not true senses, but rather instruments of sense, which put the animal in relation with the exterior world; in the service of imagination they transmit to their mistress impressions received by them from without, sensations which are transmitted to us from the objects by which we are surrounded. Imagination is the collective sense in which are united our various senses: in reality it is that which hears and which sees; it is through it that all the perceptions occur; and it assigns to each organ its particular function. From it all the faculties proceed: they are like the rays which go out of the centre and which meet wholly in the centre: many in progression, and one and the same in origin. The sense to which the organs are indispensable is a purely material sense; or, to speak more correctly, it is only a sense when it enters into the service of the imagination: imagination is the sense which has power of acting instantaneously without intermediaries. It has a divine character through which it approaches intuitive Intellect.

VII.

IMAGINATION IS LESS FALLIBLE THAN OUR PHYSICAL SENSES, WHICH OFTEN DECEIVE US.

We hold our physical senses in great estimation because they put us in harmony with the world; and that which we think we know the best is that which strikes our attention. But if we have only disdain for the imagination, because it is often at variance with our

*Literally: "Is the first body of the soul."

senses, we must not forget that the eye itself frequently deceives us; at one time it does not perceive things, at others it sees them not as they really are, because of the medium through which they are seen. According to the distance things appear larger or smaller; when in water they seem greater, and refraction frequently makes a straight ray appear broken. Sometimes moreover the eye suffers, and everything to it appears dim and confused. In the same way when the imagination is diseased do not expect clear and distinct visions.

What is the nature of these maladies? From whence come the imperfections which imagination contracts? How can it recover and regain health? A profound philosopher alone is able to tell us, and prescribe the sacred remedies which can cure the imagination and again render it divine. But in order that God may come and visit it, it is necessary that it first expell all the foreign impressions which it has received. When we live in conformity to nature, imagination remains pure and undefiled; it watches all its energies; it is thus that it approaches truly to the soul: it then enters into relation with the latter; it is then no longer a stranger to the soul, as is our corporeal envelope, upon which the beneficent influence of the spiritual principle does not act. Imagination is the vehicle of the soul. and according as the latter inclines more toward virtue or vice, is more subtile and ætherial or heavier and more terrestrial. It occupies the mean between the existence endowed with and existence deprived of reason—between spirit and matter—it serves them as a medium, and thus unites the two extremes: that is why its nature cannot be seized with exactness by the philosopher.

VIII.

IMAGINATION HAS BEEN BESTOWED UPON A MULTITUDE OF EXISTENCES, AND IT IS THROUGH IT THAT WE FORM OUR THOUGHTS.

Closely allied to matter and spirit, imagination borrows from each as to it seems expedient, and, while guarding its own nature, forms its conceptions from most opposite elements. The imaginative essence has been shared with a multitude of existences; it descends even to animals devoid of intelligence: then it is no longer the chariot upon which the divine soul is seated; it is only itself which is seated upon the inferior faculties. It holds in the breast the place of reason; it feels and acts sufficiently through itself.* With certain animals it is purified and perfected. There are a multitude of dæmons of which the existence is wholly imaginative: these are only phantoms of which the apparitions are connected with contingent things. In man imagination can do much through its inherent virtue, and much more through its association with intellect. We are able to form thoughts only with the aid of imagination, unless perhaps in short instants during which some men at once seize the truth.† To wholly transcend the imagination is a thing not less beautiful than difficult. Happy the man to whom the years bring intelligence and wisdom, said Plato, when speaking of pure wisdom.‡ But ordinary life is dominated by imagination, or by intelligence using imagination as an instrument.

IX.

IN THIS WORLD IMAGINATION HAS BEEN ASSOCIATED WITH THE SOUL; SOMETIMES IT COMMANDS THE LATTER AND AT OTHER TIMES OBEYS IT.

This breathing animal, which the wise have called a

*Imagination in that condition is only instinct.

†The most subtile and highest form of thought is intuition, but we cannot formulate this into ideas without the assistance of imagination.

‡See the Philebos.

soul endowed with breath, takes all species of forms and becomes a god, a dæmon, a phantom, in whom the soul receives the punishment for its faults. The oracles agree in saying that the soul will have in the other world an existence conforming to the visions which sleep now brings to it,* and philosophy assures us that all our present life is only a preparation for the life which is to follow. Virtuous, the soul renders the imagination lighter: it crushes it under the weight of its stains. Naturally imagination raises itself above, when it is endowed with heat and dryness: these are its wings, such is the meaning which it is essential to attach to the expressions of Herakleitos, when he says, that the soul truly wise is brilliant and dry; on the contrary, when it is thick and humid, imagination is drawn by its weight towards the lower regions, into the subterranean depths, the abode of the bad spirits; there it endures, in punishments, an unhappy existence: however, in time and with much effort it can in another life purify itself, and rise again towards heaven. At its entrance into life two roads open before it; it goes some times in the good road, and at others in the bad;† then comes the soul, which descending from the celestial sphere‡ takes hold of the imagi-

*As the ideas which still pursue us in our sleep are those which have occupied us during our waking hours, they will still continue in the other life.

†The idea of the two roads is very ancient. See the oldest Church Manual, called the Teaching of the Twelve Apostles, etc., by Phillip Schaff, New York, 1885, p. 18 sq. The Teaching of the Twelve Apostles with illustrations from the Talmud, etc., by Charles Taylor, D. D. London, 1886.

‡This idea is also very ancient. It is set forth in the Republic of Plato (*circa* 428-429, B. C.) in the narration of Er the Pamphylian, and is also in the Republic of Cicero (b. 106, d. 43, B. C.) in the dream of Scipio; a commentary on which may be found in the writings of Macrobius (b. *circa* 376, d. 420, A. D.) The Hebrew Qabbalah has the same idea. Compare the prayer of El'yahu in the Tiq-qooneh ha-Zohar, also *Disputatio Cabalistica*, etc., by Joseph De Voisin. Paris (1635. pp. 277-279.) He quotes from Plotinos to the same effect The idea most probebly came from the ancient Chaldeans, at least Pausanias strongly implies it. The Mysteries of Mithra also had some connection with it Compare also "The Face in the Moon's Orb" by Plutarch, likely a relic of the religious philosophy of the Druids. The Manichæans also held similar views.

nation; it (the soul) uses it as a chariot, in order that it may accomplish its journey in the physical world; and it (the soul) strives to lead it back to the higher regions, or at least not to remain borne down with it (the soul) in matter. Without doubt it is difficult for them to separate; sometimes, however, when the imagination will not obey, the soul liberates itself from its society: for we should not disbelieve known and true mysteries. It is a disgrace for the soul to return to the intelligible sphere if she neglects to restore that which is alien to her true nature, and leaves about the earth what she had received from on high.

Thanks to the initiations and the divine favor, there are some men who attain to the redemption of their souls from the bonds of imagination; but usually if once united they keep together, and the soul is either drawn by or it draws the imagination; and their associations continues until the time when the soul returns to the place from which it has been separated. When the imagination falls under the weight of its miseries it draws down in its fall the soul which has not known how to preserve it. This is the danger which the oracles point out to the intelligent principle which is within us:

> "Do not drag it down into this muddy world,
> Into its deep gulfs, its sad and black kingdoms,
> Sombre hideous hells, entirely peopled with phantoms."*

Indeed an unreasoning and stupid existence is not worthy to have intelligence; but the phantom, because of the elements which compose it, enjoys itself in the lower regions because the similar seeks only the similar.

X.

IF THE SOUL PERMITS ITSELF TO BE SUBDUED BY THE ATTRACTION OF MATTER IT BECOMES UNHAPPY.

If in this union intelligence becomes entirely con-

*Sibylline Oracles.

founded with imagination, it plunges into an intoxication of the greatest voluptuousness. Now the height of evil is to cease feeling it is evil, because then one will not seek for a cure: and thus it is that we do not dream of banishing the callosities from which we no longer suffer. Repentance is an aid to return to a better life. When we are tormented with our condition we strive to leave it. To intend is to have already accomplished a half of the expiation; because then all the actions and words tend to the end. But when the will is absent, the expiatory ceremonies have no longer any meaning; in order that they keep their efficacy, it is essential that the soul be a consenting element. So the troubles which strike us on different sides are marvelously proper to establish moral order; taking the place of false joys the chagrins of life purify the soul. Even misfortunes which seem to us unmerited are useful in this, that they deliver us from a too exclusive attachment to the things of this world. It is thus that Providence reveals itself to the wise, whilst the fools will not admit that it is impossible for the soul to free itself from matter, when it has not been tried by sufferings in this world. The pleasures of this earth are then only a trap that demons lay for the soul. Others say, that on leaving this life it drinks of a beverage which causes it to forget the past: my view is that it is rather at its entrance into life that it drinks from the cup of deceitful voluptuousness, the forgetfulness of its destiny. Coming into this world* to be a servant, its service changes into slavery; without doubt it ought to a certain extent, by virtue of the laws of necessity, obey nature, but alas! seduced by the attractions of matter it resembles those unfortunates who, born free, sell themselves for a time, inflamed with the beauty of a slave; and in order to remain near that

*Literally, "entering into its first life." According to the doctrine of Metempsychosis the soul passes through a series of successive lives.

which they love accept the same master. This is our condition when we allow ourselves to be charmed with false benefits, by pleasures wholly external, which affect the body alone; we appear then to admit that matter is beautiful. Matter takes hold of our admission as if by a secret engagement which we had entered into with it; and, later, if we wish to free ourselves from it and resume our liberty it treats us as deserters, it attempts to regain possession of us, and invokes, so as to make us return under its domination, the faith due to an engagement. It is especially at this time that the soul needs energy and the divine assistance: it is not a small affair to have to break, sometimes even violently, contracted habits; because then (so destiny wills it) all the forces of matter swoop down upon the rebels so as to crush and punish them. Without doubt it is this that is meant by the labours of Herakles, which we read of in the sacred legends, and those combats which other heroes so valiantly sustain, until the day upon which they could elevate themselves to those heights where nature no more had any hold upon them. If the soul makes vain efforts so as to free itself from the walls of its prison, it falls back again on itself; we have then to sustain rude contests, because matter then treats us as enemies: it revenges itself upon us for our ineffectual attempts by rigorous punishments. Then it is no longer that mixed life, of which Homer tells us, the good and the evil, which go out of two vessels, and which Jupiter (it is still the poet who is speaking) sovereign dispenser of things in this world, distributes to men.* Never has he given us a taste of the entirely pure good, but he sometimes has given us only the evil.

XI.

THE SOUL ASSIMILATES ITSELF WITH PARTICLES OF AIR AND FIRE WHICH IT OUGHT TO CARRY AWAY WITH IT WHEN IT RETURNS TO THE HIGHER SPHERES.

In these different existences the soul ceases not to err

*Iliad. xxiv. 526 sq.

if it does not promptly return to the abode from which it came. See how vast is the course that imagination can survey. When the soul descends, as we have just said, imagination, which is heavy, falls and plunges into obscure and dark abysses; but if the soul rises, it accompanies it and follows it as far as it is permitted to rise, that is as far as the superior limits of the sublunary world. Hear what is said upon this subject by the sacred oracles: Do not throw

> "The flower of matter into the terrestrial abysses;
> The phantom has its place upon the brilliant summits."*

That summit is the opposite of the dark region. But these verses contain also another meaning which must be searched for: the soul ought not only to return to the celestial sphere from whence it came, with all which constitutes its own essence: it ought also to bear away those particles of fire and air which constitute its second essence, that of phantom, and to which it assimilated when it was descending towards the earth, before having received that earthly covering; it takes back above that air and fire with its better part: for we must not understand by "the flower of matter" the divine body.† Reason says to us, that the things which have at one time participated in a common nature and been united to it, cannot any more be entirely separated, especially when they are neighbors: thus it is that fire touches the element which is diffused around the world (*i. e.* the æther), and it is not like the earth which is in the lowest degree of the scale of existences. Admit that the better consents to be allied with that which is worse, and thus produce an immortal body mingled with mud: if the more noble of the two associates puts this body

*The Sibylline Verses.

†"The flower of matter" our author deems to be particles of air and fire. The divine body with him is imagination; this he also calls; "the first body of the soul." He considers the imagination as something very subtile yet material, corresponding perhaps to Qabbalistic *Ruach*: "The flower of matter" being the *Nepesh*, and the soul the *Neshamah* of the Qabbalah.

under subjection, the part less pure cannot resist the actionof the soul; docile and submissive it follows it faithfully. Thus it is that the imagination, this intermediary essence, in yielding to the direction of the soul, the superior essence, far from changing itself, purifies itself and rises with it (the soul) towards heaven. If there are limits which it cannot pass, at least it elevates itself above the elements, and reaches to the luminous spaces; for, as the oracles say, it has its place in the brilliant region, *i. e.* the circular vault which surrounds us. But we have spoken sufficiently of the loans which the imagination makes to the elements: you can grant or refuse your belief as to this dogma; but that which is certain is, that the corporeal essence which comes from on high ought necessarily, when the soul returns to its principle, raise itself and also take its flight and join itself to the celestirl spheres; that is to say, return to its own nature.

XII.

THE TWO DIFFERENT DESTINIES OF THE SOUL AND THE IMAGINATION.

There are then two destinies opposed to each other, one obscure, the other brilliant; one the height of happiness, the other the excess of misery. But between these two extreme limits, in this sublunary world, there are, do you not think it? a great number of intermediary stations which are neither the light nor the darkness. The soul with the imagination can go over all this space, changing its state, habits and life, according to its location. When it returns to its original nobleness, it is the receptacle of truth, pure, brilliant, incorruptible, it is divine, and in order to be able to see the future has only to wish it. But when it falls into the lower regions, it contains only darkness, uncertainty and deceit for the imagination in obscuring itself becomes incapable of discerning things clearly. When it is between the two extreme points, the soul has one part truth, the other part, error. Thus it is that we can determine to which degree of the ladder the different dæmons are placed. For to remain always or nearly always in the truth, is the property of the divine or quasi-divine being; but to deceive themselves without cessation, when they endeavor to forsee the future, is the lot of those who themselves wallow in matter, blinded by their haughty passions. The dæmons who retain celestial bonds, become gods or spirits of a superior order; they raise themselves, and go to occupy the region prepared for the most noble essences.

XIII.

HOW WE ARE ABLE TO PURIFY THE SOUL AND IMAGINATION. THE EXCELLENCE OF CONTEMPLATION.

In that way we can predict what place the human soul occupies. A man in whom the imagination, pure and well regulated, perceives whilst awake or asleep only faithful images of things, can be tranquil as to the state or condition of his soul; it is the best condition. Now it is especially after visions which imagination itself forms and to which it clings, whilst it is not under the influence of exterior objects, that we are able to recognize the tendencies in which it finds itself. It is for philosophy to teach us what care it is necessary to give our imagination, and how we can preserve it from all error. The best of all preparations is, to practice especially speculative virtue of that kind which will make life a continual intellectual progression. It is necessary to as much as possible prevent the blind and disordered movements of our imagination; in other words, lean towards the good and forsake the evil, not mixing ourselves more with terrestrial things than the necessity requires. There is nothing so efficacious as contemplation to disperse the enemies who besiege the spirit. The spirit is refined by this more than we would think, and turns towards God; then, suitably prepared, it attracts by a species of affinity the divine spirit; it makes it enter into intercourse with the soul. But when it is thickened, contracted and dwarfed to the point of not being able any more to fill the place destined for it by Providence when It formed man, (I intend by that the habitation of the brain), as nature abhors a vacuum, it introduces into us an evil spirit. And what sufferings does this detestable guest bring to us! Because, since these habitations have been made to receive the spirit, nature desires that they should always be occupied by a spirit, good or wicked. This last condition is the punishment of the impious who have soiled that which they had in them which was divine; the other is even the end or nearly the end of a pious life.

XIV.

IN ORDER TO OBTAIN POSSESSION OF THE KNOWLEDGE OF DIVINATION BY DREAMS, IT IS FROM THE BEGINNING NECESSARY TO BE CHASTE AND TEMPERATE.

We have wished, in studying divination by dreams, to prove that this science is not to be despised, but on the contrary merits study, so that we may obtain all the advantages that can be drawn from it, and it is necessary to examine what is the nature of imagination. But of what use this divination can be in ordinary life we have not yet shown. The best profit that we are able to obtain, is to render the spirit healthy, and raise the soul; also it is religious exercise which renders us apt at divination. Many in their desire to forsee the future have renounced the excesses of the table so as to live sober and temperate lives; they have kept their bed pure and chaste: for the man who desires to make his bed like the tripod of Delphi will watch himself well from rendering it a witness of noctural debauches; he prostrates himself before God to pray. Thus little by little he makes provision for admirable virtues; he attains an aim more elevated than the purpose he desired, and without having at first dreamed of it he comes to attach and unite himself to God.

XV.

DIVINATION THROUGH DREAMS IS PRECIOUS AND EASY.

It is then necessary that we do not neglect divination; for it conducts us towards the divine summits, and puts in play the most precious of our faculties.

The intercourse of the soul with God does not render it less fit for the affairs of this life; its noble aspirations do not make us forget the animal existence. From an elevated position it sees more clearly all that which is below it, than if it lived confined in that inferior region; without losing any of its serenity, it gives to the animal part exact representations of all that which is produced in this contingent world.

The proverb, "descend without descending," is especially true of him who, lowering his thoughts towards objects less dignified than himself, does not keep them fixed there. This science of divination I desire to possess and bequeath to my children. In order to acquire it there is no need to undertake at great cost a painful journey, nor a long voyage, to go to Delphos or into the desert of Ammon; it is sufficient to sleep after having made ablutions and a prayer. Observe the Penelope of Homer:

> "Going out of the pure water,
> Covering her body with a veil of dazzling whiteness
> She invoked Minerva."*

We should as she did so as to taste sleep. Are you in the right condition? God, who holds himself afar, comes to you. You have no need to give yourself trouble: He presents himself always during your sleep.† In sleep, the whole business of initiation is

*Odyssey, XVII., 48.

†The Zohar holds that whenever man is asleep his *Neshamah* *i. e.* Intellectual Soul, returns to the higher place, the Garden of Eden, from which it originally came down.

performed. Never has a poor man been able to complain that his poverty hindered him from being initiated as well as the rich. Some Hierophants cannot be taken, as are the trierarchs of Athens, from amongst those who possess great fortunes; because it is necessary to spend much in order to obtain the Cretan herb, a bird of Egypt, a bone of Iberia, and other rarities of that kind which are only found in the depths of the earth and the sea, on the shores "Where the sun begins and finishes its course."*

External divination then demands costly preparations; and who is the individual sufficiently wealthy to incur all these expenses? But if it be a question of dreams, it matters little if one possesses five hundred or three hundred *medimns*, *i. e.* measures, of income;† he may be in a modest condition or even till the ground to gain a living: boatmen, hirelings, citizens, strangers, are all equal in this. God has not made any difference beween the race of Eteobutadæ and the last of the slaves. Thanks to its character divination by dreams is placed within the reach of all: plain and without artifice, it is pre-eminently rational; holy, because it does not make use of violent methods, it can be exercised anywhere; it dispenses with fountain, rock and gulf, and it thus is that which is truly divine. To practice it there is no need of neglecting any of our occupations, or to rob our business for a single moment, and that is the advantage I should have described at first. No one is advised to quit his work and go to sleep, especially to have dreams. But as the body cannot resist prolonged night-watches, the time that nature has ordained for us to consecrate to repose brings us, with sleep, an accessory more precious than sleep itself: that natural necessity becomes a source of enjoyment and we do not sleep merely to live, but to learn to live well.

*Odyssey, p 24.

†A *medimnus* contained 1¼ bushels or 12 imperial gallons.

On the contrary, divination which is exercised by the aid of material means takes the greatest part of our time, and it is a happiness if it leaves us some hours of liberty for our necessities and business. It is very rare that it is of any usefulness to us in the ordinary affairs of life; because the circumstances, the places, do not lend themselves to the accomplishment of the necessary ceremonies; and besides it is not easy to carry with us everywhere an equipage of instruments. Indeed, without speaking of the inconveniences, all this baggage, which lately the narrow walls of a prison could not contain,* would be a load for a wagon or a ship. Add again that these ceremonies have witnesses, who are able to reveal them, as it has happened in our time: so also, obeying legal prescriptions, many of the people have divulged these mysteries, and have delivered them up to the gaze and ears of the profane multitude. Beyond that it is humiliating to see the knowledge debased, that species of divination should be held in abhorrence by God. Really not to await that of which we desire the presence to come freely, but to press it, to harass it so as to draw it to us, is violence, and is to commit a fault of the nature of those that even our human laws do not leave unpunished. All this is grave; but it is not all: when we employ, in order to perceive the future, artificial means, we run the risk of being interrupted in our operations; and if we travel, leave our knowledge in our house; for it is no little matter to pack up this thing and carry it away. But in divination by dreams, each of us is in himself his proper instrument; whatever we may do, we cannot separate ourselves from our oracle: it dwells with us; it follows us everywhere, in our journeys, in war, in public office, in agricultural pursuits, in commercial enterprises.

*The Emperors, after they became Christians, interdicted superstitious practices. Synesios is here speaking of the seizure of the instruments which were used in these practices.

The laws of a jealous Republic do not interdict that divination: if they did they could do nothing: because how can the offense be proven? What harm is there in sleeping? No tyrant is able to carry out an edict against dreams, still less proscribe sleep in his dominions; that would be at once fully to command the impossible, and an impiety to put himself in opposition to the desires of nature and God.

XVI.

IT BRINGS TO ALL THE JOYS OF HOPE.

Then let all of us deliver ourselves to the interpretation of dreams, men and women, young and old, rich and poor, private citizens and magistrates, inhabitants of the town and of the country, artisans and orators. There is not any privileged, neither by sex, neither by age, nor fortune or profession. Sleep offers itself to all: it is an oracle always ready, and an infallible and silent counseller; in these mysteries of a new species each is at the same time priest and initiate. It, as well as divination, announces to us the joys to come, and, through the anticipated happiness which it procures for us, it gives to our pleasures a longer duration; and it warns us of the misfortunes that threaten us, so that we may be put on our guard. The charming promises of hope so dear to man, the foreseeing calculations of fear, all come to us through dreams. Nothing is more qualified in its effect to nourish hope in us; this good, so great and so precious that without it we could not be able, as said the most illustrious Sophists, to support life; for who would desire to remain always in the same condition? Surrounded by so much evil, man would soon allow himself to be discouraged, if Prometheus had not put in man's heart the hope which charms his pains, and gives him with forgetfulness of the present the certainty of a better future. Such is the strength of illusion that the prisoner, whose feet are held captive in the shackles, as soon as he lets his thoughts wander, sees freedom; he is a soldier, he commands half a cohort; he becomes centurion, general; he is victorious; offers sacrifices, and crowns himself so as to celebrate his triumph; he gives feasts in which shine if he chooses all the luxury of Sicily and Persia; he dreams no more of his irons, all the time that it pleases him to be a general. These reveries come even in our waking hours as in our sleep; but it is always the imagination which precedes them. Imagination, when set in play by our will, renders us the unique service of charming our existence, of offering to our soul the flattering illusions of hope, and thus consoling us for our pains.

XVII.

DREAMS ARE VERACIOUS BUT IT IS NECESSARY TO KNOW HOW TO COMPREHEND THEM.

But when dreaming brings to us from itself hope, as it comes during sleep, then we are able to consider God as the surety of the promises that dreams make to us. In preparing one's self to receive the benefits announced in dreams, we have a double happiness: at first because we enjoy in advance these benefits in idea; afterwards when we possess them in reality, we know how to use them as we ought; because we have seen the right employment that we should make of them. Pindar, speak- of the happy man, celebrates hope. "It is sweet," he says, "it nourishes the heart; it accompanies and animates youth, it is it especially which governs the variable spirit of mortals."* Without doubt there cannot be a question of that deceiving hope which we fabricate in ourselves when entirely awake. But all that Pindar says, is only a feeble part of the praise that we can render to dreams. Divination by dreams is a science which pursues the exact truth, and which inspires such confidence that we should not relegate it to

*Fragments.

an inferior rank. If the Penelope of Homer tells us that two different gates allow the passage of dreams, and that one permits the escape of deceiving dreams,* it is because she lacks a correct knowledge of the nature of dreams: better instructed she would have made them all go out of the door of horn. She is convicted of error and ignorance, when she refuses to believe a vision which ought nevertheless to inspire her with confidence. "The geese are the wooers, and the eagle that was is Ulysses."†

Ulysses was near her, and it is to him that she was speaking of the falseness of his dream. Homer evidently desired to show by this, that we must not challenge dreams, and that, if we do not deceive ourselves in our dreams, the dream itself is not deceptive. Agamemnon also was wrong in believing that a dream was false: he did not understand the prophesy that foretold victory for him:

> "Order all the Greeks to put on their arms,
> And the walls of Ilion will fall before thee."‡

He then marched, supposing that the city would fall at the first assault; but the prophesy said that it was necessary that *all* the Greeks should arm themselves. Now Achilles and the troop of Myrmidons, the very flower of the army, refused to take part in the combat.

XVIII.

THE OBLIGATIONS OF SYNESIOS TO DREAMS.

But dreams have been sufficiently eulogized; let us stop. But I must not be ungrateful. I have already shown that, travelling the seas or resting at firesides,

*"There are two portals of unsubstantial dreams: one is made of horn, one of ivory; whichever come througn the sawn ivory deceive and bring promises which will never be fulfilled; but those which come out of the doors of the polished horn bring a true issue when any one of mortals sees them." Odyssey, XIX., 562.

†Odyssey, XIX., 548.

‡Iliad, II., 11.

be you merchants or soldiers, always and everywhere we carry with us the faculty of foreseeing the future. But I have not yet stated my own indebtedness to dreams. And yet it is to the minds given to Philosophy that dreams especially come, to enlighten them in their difficulties and researches, so as to bring them during sleep the solutions which escape them when awake. We seem in sleeping at one time to apprehend, at another to find, through our own reflection. As for me, how often dreams have come to my assistance in the composition of my writings! Often have they aided me to put my ideas in order, and my style in harmony with my ideas; they have made me expunge certain expressions, and choose others. When I allowed myself to use images and pompous expressions, in imitation of the new Attic style, so far removed from the old, a god warned me in my sleep, censured my writings, and making the affected phrases disappear, brought me back to a natural style. At other times, in the hunting season, I invented, after a dream, traps to catch the swiftest animals and the most skillful in hiding. If, discouraged from too long waiting, I was preparing to return to my home, dreams would give me courage, by announcing to me, for such or such a day, a better result: I then patiently watched some nights more; many animals would fall in my nets or under my arrows. All my life has been spent among books or in hunting, except the time of my embassy: and would to the gods I had never lived those three cursed years! But then again divination has been singularly useful to me: it preserved me from ambushes that certain magicians laid for me, revealed their sorceries and saved me from all danger; it sustained me during the whole duration of the mission which has caused to prosper the greatest good in the cities of Libyia; it conducted me even before the Emperor, in the midst of his court, in which I have spoken with an independence, of which no Greek ever before had given an example.

XIX.

WHEREFORE DREAMS ARE SELDOM LUCID, AND WHEREFORE ART IS NEEDED TO EXPLAIN THEM.

Each kind of divination has its particular adepts; but divination by dreams addresses itself to all. It offers itself to each of us as a propitious divinity; it adds new conceptions to those which we have found in our waking meditations. Nothing is wiser than a soul disengaged from the tumult of the senses, which only bring to it from without troubles without end. The ideas that it possesses, and, when it is wrapped in itself, those that it receives from intelligence, it communicates to those who are turned towards the interior life; it makes all that which is from God enter into them; because between that soul and the divinity which animates the world there exist intimate affinities, because both come from the same source. Dreams then have nothing earthly; they are clear and give a perfect or nearly perfect evidence; there is no need of an interpreter. But this happiness is reserved only to those who live in the practice of virtue, acquired by an effort of reason or by habit. It is very rarely that other men have such lucid dreams; sometimes this happens, but only in very grave conjectures. At other times their dreams are vulgar and confused and full of obscurity: it is necessary to have the aid of art in order to explain them. As their origin is, so to say, strange and fantastic, by virtue of that origin they only offer uncertainty.

XX.

ALL THINGS PAST, PRESENT AND FUTURE CONVEY TO US IMAGES WHICH ARE REFLECTED IN OUR IMAGINATION.

All things which exist in nature, which have existed, which will exist (because the future is yet a mode of existence), send out images which escape from their substance. Perceptible objects are composed of form and matter:* now, as we see that matter is a perpetual condition of motion, and that the images which it produces are borne away by it, we are forced to admit this; thus images and matter, all that which falls into generation, does not approach in dignity permanent existence (*real* being). All these fugitive images reflect themselves in the imagination as in a brilliant mirror. Wandering at random and detached from the objects in which they have taken existence, as they have only an undecided existence, and as none of the beings who exist by themselves will receive them, when they meet animal spirits who themselves are also images† but from images residing in us, they penetrate into these spirits, they establish themselves there as in a dwelling. Things passed, since they have been realities, give clear images, which finish at length by effacing themselves and disappearing; present things, as they continue to exist, form images still more clear and living; but the future gives us nothing except vagueness and indistinctness: so from the buds, which have just made their appearance, we surmise the flowers and leaves, as yet badly formed, which they contain and which will open and burst out in a short time. Thus art is indispensable in order to know the future; we can only have an uncertain sketch of that which is to come; we have only in exact representation that which is.

XXI.

IT IS NECESSARY BY MEANS OF PHILOSOPHY TO KEEP OUR IMAGINATION FREE FROM THE PASSIONS.

But is it not astonishing that it can itself produce

*This idea is fully set forth in the works of Solomon Ibn Gebirol or Avicebron, especially in his *Me-qor Hay-yeem*, i. e., Source of Life. It is a doctrine also set forth with great positiveness in the Zohar and the Hebrew Qabballah.

†*Εἰδώλοις*. This word has the double meaning of images and phantoms.

images of that which will be only later? It is here that I ought to speak of how we can acquire that art of divination. That which is first necessary is that the divine spirit which is in us be sufficiently prepared, so as to be visited by intelligence and by God, and not be the receptacle of vain images. Now, when this (the latter) happens, we should take refuge in philosophy, whose beneficial action appeases the passions which besiege the spirit and invade it so as to make it their dwelling. Foster in your life habits of temperance and frugality, so as not to agitate the animal part of your existence: the troubles of the senses extend even to the imagination, which must be kept quiet and tranquil. That calmness is very easy to be desired but very difficult to obtain. For myself, as I wish that sleep be not useless to any one, I will try and discover a fixed rule which is applicable to the infinite variety of dreams; in other words, it is my object to establish a science of the nocturnal appearances. Here is how we can undertake it.

XXII.

HOW WE CAN UNDERTAKE THE INTERPRETATION OF DREAMS.

The navigator who, after having passed a rock, perceives a city, knows afterwards, when he sees the same rock that the same city will soon be in sight. We have no need to see a General in order to know that he is coming, his approach becomes known to us by the escort which precedes him: because each time it has appeared, it was because the General was coming. So images which present themselves to our spirit are *indicia* of the future; the return of the same signs predict the return of the same events. He is a stupid pilot who repasses near the same rock without recognizing it, and who cannot tell what shore he is near; he navigates at random. So the man who has dreamed the same dream several times, and who has not observed what this dream predicts—accident, happiness, undertaking,—he directs his life as that pilot directs his vessel, without reflection. We prognosticate storms even when everything in the atmosphere is tranquil, if we observe circles around the moon; because we have often noticed that this phenomenon is frequently followed by a storm:

> A single circle, fading, denotes fine weather;
> If it is broken, it certainly announces wind,
> If it is double, believe me, a tempest is near;
> But if it is triple, and dark, and broken, I expect
> Then more than ever, the fury of storms.*

Thus always, as Aristotle has said† with reason, perception precedes memory, from memory comes experience and from experience knowledge. It is by this means that we come to the interpretation of dreams.

XXIII.

ON ACCOUNT OF THE DIVERSITY OF MINDS THERE IS NO GENERAL RULE FOR THE EXPLANATION OF DREAMS.

There are men who use many books in which are set forth the rules of this art. Personally I ignore these books, and regard them as useless. For though the last or lowest body, which is a composition of different elements, cannot by reason of its nature be an object of a knowledge which is one and positive, since the affections which it experiences are produced nearly always alike, and through the same causes, (because the elements constituting it differ very little from each other, and the difficulties which trouble the organism cannot remain concealed), it is not thus with imagination. Here it is entirely a different thing: between different spirits there exist great differences, according as they are connected with the spheres or reign over matter.

*Aratos: Prognostics, 81.
†Metaphysics, I. 1.

Happy in this world, among all the souls,
Is the soul which has descended from the ethereal heights,
The soul also, which knew Jupiter's Court,
And which living here below contains its destiny,
Even in this exile remains nevertheless happy.

It was this which Timæus signified, when he assigned a star to each soul. But souls have lapsed: inflamed through material desires they have fallen more or less below, and in their fall the imagination has been defiled. So sunk they inhabit bodies: life is now one long discord; the spirit is sick: an unnatural condition if we consider its noble origin, but natural as to the animal existence with which it is connected, and which it animates. Perhaps however the nature of the spirit depends entirely on the rank which it occupies, according to its practice of vice or virtue. For there is nothing so variable as the spirit. How, with dissimilar natures obeying different laws and passions, are there the same apparitions? That is not so; it cannot be. Water, muddy or clear, tranquil or agitated, can it equally reflect objects? Vary its tints, move it in different ways, the figures will change in appearance; they will only have one characteristic in common, that of deviating from the true. If this is contested,—if some Phemonoe, some Melampos, or other diviner pretends to establish, for the explanation of dreams, a general rule, we would ask him if plane or convex mirrors, or those made of different materials, reflect similar images. But never, I think, have these people considered the nature of spirit. As the imagination is akin to the spirit in a certain respect, they apprehend that there is one rule and canon for the interpretation of all things. I do not claim that between things most dissimilar there is absolutely no relation; but this relation is obscure, and becomes more obscure if it is unduly extended. Add, as I have said, that it is difficult to have a clear image of future things before they come into actual existence.

Finally, as we all have our idiosyncrasies, it is not possible that the same visions should have the same signification for all.

XXIV.

EACH OUGHT TO MAKE HIS DIVINATORY KNOWLEDGE FOR HIMSELF, BY NOTING HIS DREAMS.

We must not hope then to establish general rules: each one must search for his knowledge within himself. We should inscribe in our memory all that has come to us in our dreams. It is easy to do that which is entire-profitable; the profit which it brings is a stimulant, especially when we have that which we exercise. What is more usual than dreams? What exercises a stronger influence on the mind? Such an influence, indeed, that evèn the dullest give attention to their dreams. It is a disgrace, at twenty-five years of age, to still need an interpreter for one's dreams, and not to possess the principles of this art. For the memories which should have carefully kept the visions of our sleep as well as the events which happen when we are awake certainly have their value. It is a novelty which will perhaps shock received ideas: but nevertheless, wherefore should we not completɘ the history of our days with that of our nights, and so retain a remembrance of our dual lives? There is a life of the imagination, as we have demonstrated, sometimes better, sometimes worse, than ordinary life, according as the spirit is healthy or sick. If then we are carful in noting our dreams, while thus acquiring the knowledge of divination, we will not let anything escape our memory, and we will have pleasure in composing this biography, which will give our history both waking and sleeping. Moreover, if we desire to become rhetoricians, we can find no better method for the development of the oral faculties. When we commit our daily impressions to writing, as we neglect no details, and note little things as well as great, we habituate ourselves, says the sophist of Lemnos,* to successfully treat all subjects. But what an admirable theme does the history of our nightly visions furnish to the orator!

XXV.

DREAMS BRING TO THE MIND ALL KINDS OF IMAGES AND IMPRESSIONS.

It is not an easy thing to set forth exactly all the circumstances of a dream, to separate that which is found united by nature and to unite that which is separated, and give to others, by our descriptions. dreams which they have not had. It is no easy work to make our own impressions pass into the soul of another. Imagination relegates into nothingness beings which exist; it causes to proceed from nothing beings which do not exist, which cannot exist. How, at a time when we have no idea of anything similar, can we represent objects which it is impossible for us even to name? Imagination assembles many images at the same time, and presents them at the same instant, but confused, such as the dream gives them; for it is according to the dream that our visions are produced. In order to faithfully render these various impressions all the resources of language are necessary. Imagination acts upon our affections more than one would think: dreams excite different emotions in us; we at one time experience sentiments of sympathy and attachment, at another aversion. It is also during sleep that the enchantments of magic exercise themselves upon us, and that we are especially subject to voluptuousness; love and hate penetrate into our souls, and persist in remaining even after our awaking.

XXVI.

VARIOUS MARVELS ARE PRESENTED TO US BY DREAMS.

If we would communicate to our hearers our impressions and ideas, a lively and forcible language is essen-

*Philostratos.

tial. In dreams, one is a conqueror, we walk, we fly. Imagination lends itself to all; have words the same facilities? Sometimes we dream that we sleep, that we are dreaming, that we arise, that we shake off sleep, and yet we are asleep; we reflect on the dream we have just had; even that is still a dream, a double dream; we think no more of recent chimeras; we imagine ourselves now awake, and we regard the present visions as if realities. Thus is produced in our mind a veritable combat; we think that we make an effort for ourselves, that we have driven away the dream, that we are no longer asleep, that we have taken the full possession of our being, and that we have ceased to be the dupe of an illusion. The Aloidæ, for attempting to climb to heaven, by heaping one upon another the mountains of Thessaly, were punished; but what law forbids a sleeper from rising above the earth upon wings surer than those of Icarus, from excelling the flight of eagles, from soaring above the celestial sphres? We perceive the earth from afar, we discover a world which even the moon does not see. We can talk with the stars, mingle with the invisible company of the gods who rule the universe. These marvels which cannot be readily described, are nevertheless accomplished without the least effort. We enjoy the presence of the gods without being exposed to jealousy. Without having the trouble of redescending, we find ourselves upon the earth; for one of the privileges of our dreams is the suppression of time and space. Then we talk with sheep: their bleating becomes a clear and distinct language. Is there not therefore a vast field opened to an eloquence of a new kind? From whence came the apologue which makes the peacock, the fox, and even the sea speak? These audacities of imagination are insignificant when compared with the temerity of dreams; but, although the apologue is only a very feeble reproduction of some of our dreams, it furnishes nevertheless ample material for oratorical talent. Why should we not exercise ourselves in interpreting dreams? By this one not only trains himself in the art of oratory, but also gains wisdom.

XXVII.

IT IS MUCH MORE USEFUL TO TAKE OUR DREAMS FOR THE TEXTS OF OUR LITERARY EXERCISES, THAN THE RIDICULOUS SUBJECTS CHOSEN BY MANY OF THE RHETORICIANS.

Let us then employ our leisure in telling the events which happen to us whilst awake or during sleep; consecrate to this work a portion of your time and from it you will derive, as I have shown, inestimable advantages. You will acquire the science of divination which we have eulogized, and above which we cannot place anything: elegance of diction, something not to be despised, will likewise come to you. In this kind of work the philosopher unbends his mind as the Scythian unbends his bow. Dreams also furnish to the rhetoricians admirable texts for their showy discourses. I can scarcely comprehend what interest they find in celebrating the virtues of Miltiades, of Cimon, or even some anonymous person: in making the rich speak and the poor struggle with each other about public affairs. I have nevertheless seen old men wrangling on these subjects at the theatre; and such old men! They made a show of philosophical gravity, and wore a beard which might well, I imagine, weigh several pounds. But their gravity did not hinder them from insulting each other, from getting the better of each other, from supporting, with extravagant gestures, their long discourses. It seemed to me that they were pleading the cause of some parent: but what a surprise when I afterwards learned that the persons whom they were defending, far from being of their family, did not even exist, had never existed, and could not exist! Is there a republic which, to recompense the services of a citizen, permits him to kill his enemy?* When at the age of ninety years they are still disputing on such pitiable inventions, at what time of life will they take up serious work and discourses? Do these people then not know the meaning of words? They are ignorant that declamation involves preparatory exercises; they take the means for the end, the road for the goal which it is necessary to to attain. They make even the preparation the sole object of all their efforts. To bend the arms in the exercises of the *palæstra*, is that sufficient in order to be proclaimed conqueror in the *pancratium*† in the Olympic games? Scarcity of thoughts but abundance of words is what characterizes these people—always ready to speak, even when they have nothing to say. Why not profit by the example of Alkaios and Archilochos, who narrated their own lives? In this way the memory of those things which happened to them—whether pleasant or painful—was preserved for posterity. Neither did they record vain and unprofitable things, as the new race of wits who practice themselves on imaginary subjects. Neither have these wits consecrated their genius to the glory of others, like Homer and Stesichoros, who have added by their poems to the celebrity of heroes, and who excite our souls to virtue, entirely in forgetfulness of themselves. All we know of them is that they were excellent poets. So then if you wish to make a name for yourselves with posterity, if you feel yourself capable of bringing forth a work which may live forever, do not hesitate to enter into the entirely new path which I recommend to you. Count on the future: the future faithfully guards that which, with the aid of God, we confide to it.

*A wealthy man and a poor man are enemies: the rich man promises to furnish food for the people, if they will authorize him to kill the poor man: this permission is granted him. But the rich man does not feed the son of the poor man, who dies of hunger.—This is the subject to which Synesios alludes.

†The *palæstra* was a place for wrestling, and probably was part of the *gymnasium*. At Athens, however, many of these places were separate from the latter. The *pancratium* was an athletic game, in which all the powers of the contestants were called into action. It was considered as one of the difficult exercises, and usually was boxing and wrestling